Pyrophytic

Sarah Lebbos

BookLeaf
Publishing

Presentation by *BookLeaf Publishing*

Web: www.bookleafpub.com

E-mail: info@bookleafpub.com

ISBN: 9789395755092

First edition 2022

DEDICATION

For Cae, without which this book would not
have been started.

For my friends and family, I love you more than
anything.

and for Joan, you deserved a softer ending.

Tullaburra

My cup is too loud as it knocks against the
bench of our borrowed kitchen. It shatters the
soft silence that has been settling in the room
overnight, warm and surrounding.

You are still asleep; I can see the shape of you
outlined by blankets through the partially open
door to your room.

You took the smaller one, although I know you
wanted the bigger. We could have shared.

I made a pot of tea, although I suspect that I will
drink it all before you are awake. The second pot
always tastes like the earth with this tea. I dig
my fingers into the soil, wrap them around the
mug. The morning begins.

Matu

We lay there in the quiet of night.
The soft silence that weighs delightfully on a
room
when the people within are happy to let it linger.
Hand to calf, head to thigh,
curling into each other with the ease that comes
to friends.
Or family.
And a fondness seeps in,
Shone in the candlelight, and in the faces it
reflects.
It pools in my chest, spreads to my fingers as
they card through hair,
My stomach as someone refills my tea cup,
My lips breaking into a grin.
I am soft and warm and so full of love.
Let's stay here a little longer.

Bloom

For you I would grow flowers born from soft
aches and sun bright grins.
Break open my ribs and dig my fingers into the
soil, plant bulbs of soft looks and softer voices.
Creation is gentle really, when it is born of
affection. My soil stained hands find their place
in yours.
Creation is everything really, when you create
yourself. And tonight, everything I am is in
bloom.

For Freckling

Your mother guards her name,
And quite right too,
precious things should be guarded.
You, little one, are more precious still,
Yet your name sits on my tongue, wishing to
burst from my lips.
I know you by your hand,
And by your name,
And by the stories your mother tells me.
You, sweet girl, who are wrapped in cloth from
across the globe
Have seen flowers that will never grow in your
yard.
As you will never grow in mine.
Darling freckling, as you grow,
Like a sapling unfurling from a long awaited
seed,
Know that you are loved.

Kamal

My Gido had the best fruit trees.
His apricots were golden sweet,
Juice dripping down the chin.
As a child I climbed the fig trees in the
backyard,
Swinging from branches and chasing the best
ones before the birds could get them.
Mind the leaves, my father would call. Don't eat
the milk sap.
In the front he had pomegranates.
Heavy and round, we split them open
And gorged ourselves on the jewel red seeds.
There is something about working for the taste,
Pistachios split by teeth, grapes spat out by
impatient mouths.
If I could, I would brave the leaf rash of his fig
trees,
Gather a basket and wipe the milk sap from the
fruit.
I can climb higher now than I could before,
but I don't fit as well between the arms.
My Gido had the best fruit trees.
One day, I will take the seeds from his apricots
And bring them home to grow.

Kin Abba Ulami Qalb

When a language dies, its remains calcify.
And there it exists
In perfect form.
Untouched.
Our language bursts from my tongue,
Imperfect and so much better in its
imperfections,
Alive, growing,
It is reborn with every utterance.

Our language has three words for love.
Our language was built on it.

My friend writes stahabaini in the tags of a post.
Checks in with a small touch and a soft niba?
My friend's lungs breathe life into words trapped
on pages,
Gives forms with cracked smile to sounds in a
table.

When a language dies, it ceases to become.
Our language has barely just begun to grow,
Like saplings from the earth.
My friend coaxes them to bloom
and we bloom alongside them.

North

The memory is a sweet one,
A pile of cushions,
The warmth from the sun
seeping into skin, settling into bones.
A breeze carries over the hill,
And so too does the sound of music.
I fold it up, tuck it between my ribs
Let it expand in my chest
when I need to breathe a little deeper.

You came back windswept,
Eyes wild with something else
Swirling and building inside you.
Under the skin, a current, a charge, like the taste
of the air before a storm.
Like the potential curled within a seed.
And everything was moss green and lightning
silver,
Each word cast on the air like a cloud building
to rain,
Washing the land anew.

Firelight

She holds herself gently,
a flickering firelight saved from the wind
by hands cupped ever so carefully around it.
Other people's hands are never so careful.
They warm themselves by her flames,
huddle closer and press themselves against her.
And she grows, burning brighter and more
steady,
Until her fingertips are alight by it.
They marvel at her, call her beautiful, radiant.
She beams, glows with it.
It's easy, her fire is eager to burn
And so what if she is the tinder as well as flame?
So what if parts of her hollow with it?
The wind can't touch her now.

Joan

The first time she hears them she is in the
garden.
The voice is sweet and low, and asks her to be
good.
At 13, she is raised with the word of God on her
lips and flowers in her hair.
How could she be anything but?

At 17 she is struck by an arrow.
Fueled by her Lord and His grace, she storms
Orléans.
Her channeled divinity laps at the edges of her
skin like waves, pushing her ever forward.
She cannot breathe too deep for fear of
drowning in it.
The arrow hurts as it tears through her skin and
muscle.
Despite it all she is 17.
The vessel of her Lord is clay worked by holy
fingers.
Even holy, clay cracks.

They call her Maiden and Saviour,
Her name uttered by the same tongues that utter
His name with such devotion.

She sees His approval and affection in the
sunlight that falls on her armour, the cool breeze
that turns her head towards Reims and to her
king.
It is summer and she is alight.

Her king does not understand.
He calls for peace to ears that have long since
turned from holy word.
When she is struck again, it pins her, and she is
defeated at the foot of Paris.
She prays that night on bloody knees,
Her hands are clasped tight enough that they do
not tremble.

When she is 18, she is ambushed.
For 7 months she flees that tower, only to be
brought back like wave to the shore.
She leaps, still sure that He will catch her safely
as she falls.
She is alive. It is enough.

The men call themselves holy.
She laughs to herself in the long moments she is
left in her cell.
They ask her questions and misunderstand.
She answers them but they are not the judge she
cares about.

She knows the outcome of this trial as well as
she knows the outcome to His.
Joan does not fear death, but in the quiet of her
cell she might admit to herself that she fears the
flames.
It is here, alone and accused, that she turns 19.

When they tie her to the wood, she does not hear
voices.
Clay was made for the fire, she knows.
The light it casts is holy and cleansing.
Only-
Only It hurts.
She didn't think it would hurt like this
She tries to form words, prayers, but she can't
breathe
She was wrong. It's not like drowning at all.

Lessons

Fine. If she is to burn, let her burn.
If she is to be consumed, let her consume
And devour those who would dare to set her
alight.
Earth that is scorched and scarred by flame does
not forget so easily,
Nor is it unchanged by the touch of it.
The next time sweet smiles and coaxing touches
burn across her skin,
she burns them back.
Those who play with fire get burnt.
She makes sure of it.

For Joey

I hold my grief in my legs.

It weighs me down like a child, clinging to the
thighs of their caretaker with each step,
climbing to my chest and taking root in my
lungs,
an insistent pushing at the boundaries of me;
waves lapping at the shoreline of my bones.

I hold my grief in my legs because I cannot hold
it in my arms.
I hold my grief in my legs because I cannot hold
it anywhere else

Pyrophytic

The map in my head is patchwork.
The threads that connect them are not orderly,
they criss-cross at inefficient avenues,
some etched so deep, repeating over and over
again
that they stand out stark against the fabric.
The map in my head has holes, some dark and
blackened
As if someone has taken a flame to it
Burnt away at the paths until it is only a mass to
avoid.
It leaves ash on my fingertips and a foul taste in
my mouth.
I think that if I could sit with it, hold needle in
hand and try to mend what is untouchable
I would embroider little flowers.
Banksia's vibrant yellows after flame.

A short walk before we get back to work

Rain comes like relief
A chance to breathe after the heat,
Washing away the sweat and smoke.
Plants open cautiously to the sky,
Their leaves unfurling in the hope of something
to sustain them,
Bring them back to themselves.
At work the kids have done chalk drawings
The rain has made the colours run into each
other
Like too eager children on the playground.

After

And the end of it all
You have to come home.
Shed the heavy coat and put it away,
Free your feet from shoes and line them up in a
neat row.
At the end of it all there is a table and chairs,
And warm bread with butter
And tea.
And the person who made it for you,
even if that person is you.
At the end of it all you come home, and you
mind your hearth.
Let that same fire that blazes and rages through
you simmer down
And you warm your hands by it, gentle.
And you cook with it. And let it sustain you.
And the end of it all,
When the flames have licked at you,
and devoured all they can,
You have to make a home.

Of Eight

Breathless feet fall on stones lined in moss,
A ringing sound of laughter followed by
hardly-meant curses.
The damp has reached my skin now, toes curling
against the feeling even as the only thought is
flying across the path after you.
You twist, dart about, and wriggle your way
through a maze of wood, and brick, and
livelihood.
A miscalculation and I'm upon you,
I steal my shoe back, thank you very much.
I have to get home, it's getting dark. You're still
lit up from the game.
Ass ❤

Good for the Sole

There is a pair of green converse sitting on the
step,
It's colour used to be bright and stark,
a pop against the stone of the tile.
Bring them inside, my mother says, it's going to
rain.
That's the point, I tell her.
When it rains, the green deepens like it's living
The old colour returns to it and shines.
There is a flower growing between the two
shoes now,
And it too brightens when the clouds darken.
It makes me happy, I tell my mother.
On the steps they remain.

There will be enough, there will be plenty

When my grandfather was dying we were
allowed up in twos to see him.
My aunt left a box of food in his room so we
could share a meal all together,
two mouths at a time
Today was his memorial. We laid a feast.
The kids ran on the grass, among flowers,
unaware that their steps fell beside graves.
At the house they ran among flowers too,
and weaved between chairs laid at the table
I'm sorry you're hurting, I cooked for you.
I'm sorry you're hurting, I'll eat.
Meanwhile, the kids play.
Meanwhile, the flowers here grow.
I love you. Let's eat

Last: Supper

There is a certain love passed around the dinner
table,
Like bread passed from hand to hand
Torn and shared and whole and full.
There is an ache in expectant hunger and in
satisfied fullness.
In eager eyes and contented smiles.
In the creation of a thing made to be devoured.
In its devouring,
In open doors and steady flames and toasted
sandwiches late at night.
The stacked dishes and stained table cloth and
old worn marks in the furniture.
Years of meals and hunger and relief both
shared.
There is a care in recipes, passed down from the
lips of old grandmothers to willing and unused
hands.
Here is my plate to share, it says,
Here is my share
Here is me shared

www.ingramcontent.com/pod-product-compliance
Lightning Source LLC
Chambersburg PA
CBHW061326140726
47998CB00007B/2562